R. VAUGHAN WILLIAMS

THE SOLENT

EDITED BY

JAMES FRANCIS BROWN

STUDY SCORE

MUSIC DEPARTMENT

OXFORD

UNIVERSITY PRESS

OXFORD
UNIVERSITY PRESS

Great Clarendon Street, Oxford OX2 6DP,
United Kingdom

Oxford University Press is a department of the University of Oxford.
It furthers the University's objective of excellence in research, scholarship,
and education by publishing worldwide. Oxford is a registered trade mark of
Oxford University Press in the UK and in certain other countries

First published 2013

Impression: 2

ISBN 978–0–19–339941–9 (study score)
ISBN 978–0–19–339548–0 (on hire)

Music origination by Enigma Music Production Services, Amersham, Bucks.

Printed in Great Britain on acid-free paper by
Caligraving Ltd, Thetford, Norfolk

CONTENTS

PREFACE

On 19 June 1903, according to a diary entry, *The Solent* was given its first performance—the only time the work was heard until the present publication occasioned a recording and performance in 2013. The circumstances of the 1903 performance are unknown; the score itself exhibits extensive revision, with blue pencil markings understood by Michael Kennedy to result from performance preparation by Sir Henry Wood for what may have been a private play-through. So, from a somewhat obscure beginning, the score was withdrawn by the composer, and for 110 years it has roused the curiosity of Vaughan Williams scholars and admirers who have long suspected this to be a significant work in the composer's early orchestral output.

In 1902 Vaughan Williams began the composition of what he described as *Four Impressions for Orchestra*, to be titled *In the New Forest*. Only the first two movements survive from this venture, but it is just possible that the *Two Impressions for Orchestra* of 1904–7 represent the third and fourth movements and that the four 'impressions' had simply been divided. Certainly, the title of the first of the later two 'impressions', *Boldre Wood* (lost), relates to a region of the New Forest, although the second, *Harnham Down*, denotes an area that is a little too far north of the boundary.

The Solent was intended as the second of the four movements (following *Burley Heath*, which was left incomplete), and it is prefaced by the following lines from the poet Philip Bourke Marston (1850–87):

> Passion and sorrow in the deep sea's voice,
> A mighty mystery saddening all the wind?

This choice of poetry provides an illuminating subtext to the work, since these words do not, in fact, relate to the stretch of water between the mainland of Southern England and the Isle of Wight. They come instead from a poem that Marston wrote in tribute to his sister Cicely. The poet was struck by blindness at the age of four, and his sister grew to be his precious amanuensis. Sea imagery permeates the poem, invoking a companionable, reflective spirit and marking the vicissitudes of life through the passage of time, as the lines that immediately precede the above quotation suggest:

> Did we not share our sorrows and our joys
> In later years, when we awoke, to find
> Passion and sorrow...

The subject of time is perhaps a key to the resonance of this poetry for Vaughan Williams, and *The Solent* clearly held a potent significance for the composer, who returned to it several times throughout his long life. The haunting opening phrase for unaccompanied clarinet, for instance, seems to have symbolized an idyllic openness and bears a certain kinship with the horn solo of the *Pastoral Symphony* (1921). Moreover, near the beginning of *A Sea Symphony* (begun in 1903, the year of *The Solent*, and completed in 1909) the first two bars of *The Solent* emerge in majestic fashion with the words 'And on its limitless, heaving breast, the ships: See, where their white sails, bellying in the wind, speckle the green and blue...'. The theme returns in the last movement of the symphony, demonstrating its aptness as a subject of recall and evocation.

In 1955 Vaughan Williams turned again to *The Solent* for material for the film documentary *The England of Elizabeth*. *The Solent* theme accompanies images of Tintern Abbey in a rather austere unison that reminds us of the composer's profound interest in the music of the Elizabethan age as a revitalising force in twentieth-century English music. Similarly, the remote yet richly divided string writing in bars 22–9 of *The Solent*—featuring a migration from minor to major and with simple diatonic harmonies distributed so as to call forth a polyphonic resonance—clearly foreshadows the *Fantasia on a Theme by Thomas Tallis* (1910, rev. 1919).

Its final, perhaps most poignant, incarnation is in the slow movement of *Symphony No. 9* (1956–8). Here the harsh contrast between the calm of *The Solent* theme and the ominous interruptions of 'the ghostly drummer of Salisbury Plain' reminds us that two world wars and many years of creative development separate this work from its progenitor. However, the composer's programme note for the symphony reveals his diffidence concerning assumptions of a programmatic intent in his music:

> The second movement, *Andante Sostenuto*, seems to have no logical connection between its various themes. This has led some people to think that it must have a programme since apparently programme music need not be logical. It is quite true that this movement started off with a programme, but it got lost on the journey—so now, oh no, we never mention it—and the music must be left to speak for itself—whatever that may mean.

It also reveals a dismissive attitude to the earlier work:

> This theme is borrowed from an earlier work of the composer's [*The Solent*], luckily long since scrapped, but changed so that its own father would hardly recognize it.

This pejorative remark may perhaps be taken as a sign of modesty, since *The Solent* is clearly a very affecting and well-shaped work. It does not suffer from the absence of its companion pieces and may stand as a sort of tone-poem in its own right.

James Francis Brown
July 2013

MANUSCRIPT AND TEXTUAL NOTES

The full-score manuscript, in the music collection of the British Library, is bound in a single volume together with the manuscripts of *Burley Heath* and *Harnham Down* (Add. MS 57278). The title page bears the composer's address: *10 Barton St, London S.W.* At the bottom of this page, there is a handwritten note: *Withdrawn by the composer who intended to destroy the MS. Therefore not for performance, Ursula Vaughan Williams.*

The manuscript has many deletions and corrections, sometimes scratched out with a blade or else written over the original notations. Formal revisions are also apparent in several sections where the manuscript has been cut and pasted into a different order. Such instances are included in the notes below. Many notational inconsistencies deemed to be mistakes have been discreetly amended for uniformity, but where doubt arises square brackets have been used.

Throughout the manuscript there are markings in blue pencil that are supposed by Michael Kennedy to be in the hand of Sir Henry Wood. These markings relate to tempo indications and some deletions. If this is indeed the case, some of the decisions may not have been directly sanctioned by the composer.

The following bars have tempo indications in blue pencil: 1, 31, 57, 60, 67, 124, 126, 131, 136, 163, and 164.

The page numbering of the manuscript presents at least three layers of numerals, which are often re-ordered or missing. In most cases the continuity is unambiguous, but there are some instances where the inclusion of material is contextually dubious (see bars 40–2 and bar 168 of the Textual Notes).

The trumpet parts in the manuscript are for instruments in F and have here been transcribed for trumpets in B♭.

The rehearsal numbers are those marked in blue pencil in the manuscript.

The final page of music is followed by five blank pages of manuscript. On the sixth page, in blue pen, upside down as if jotted on note paper, the following text appears: *Lard-Esnault, 115 Rue Reaumur.*

1	The indication of string divisi by desk is marked in blue pencil.
24–6	MS only shows slurs in Vln 1.
38	MS: the two following bars have been roughly crossed out in blue pencil.
39	Hns, note 1: cadence supplied by editor; missing in MS.
40–1	These bars are rejoined by pasting.
40–2	MS: overlying the page with these bars is a sheet of MS attached at the top by a taped hinge. This page contains two bars of related music. The figuration in the string parts does not concur with the context, and there is a rhythmic augmentation of the descending scale (bar 40) that disturbs the formal balance. For these reasons the editor feels that this is, in fact, a discarded page of MS.
43–4	Pasted bars showing a reversal of MS page numbers 24 and 25.
63	MS: the following bar is crossed out in blue pencil.
64	MS: the four bars following this are crossed out in blue pencil. The material relates to bars 80–3.
99	Note under this bar, apparently in RVW's hand: '1 bar more?'
168	MS: following this bar, the final page of MS is attached to a binding stub, presumably by the British Library. The seven bars that follow in the MS constitute a variant of the previous five bars (164–8) and commence with an apparent non sequitur; there are unnecessary tie conclusions in the bassoons and the resultant voice-leading would be ungainly, though not entirely inconceivable. It is the editor's opinion that this represents a draft version and that the reverse of the page (bars 168 to conclusion as published) should be the final page of MS.

THE SOLENT

ORCHESTRATION

2 FLUTES

OBOE

COR ANGLAIS

2 CLARINETS

2 BASSOONS

4 HORNS (in F)

2 TRUMPETS (in B♭)

2 TENOR TROMBONES

BASS TROMBONE

TUBA

TIMPANI

STRINGS

Duration: *c*.12 minutes

Study scores of *Burley Heath* (978–0–19–339939–6) and *Harnham Down* (978–0–19–339940–2) are also available on sale, and complete orchestral material is available on hire/rental.

The Solent

"Passion and sorrow in the deep sea's voice,
A mighty mystery saddening all the wind?"
Philip Marston

R. VAUGHAN WILLIAMS

Printed in Great Britain

OXFORD UNIVERSITY PRESS, MUSIC DEPARTMENT, GREAT CLARENDON STREET, OXFORD OX2 6DP

79
Fl. 1 2
a 2
f p
p
5
Ob.
Solo
p
C. A.
Cl. (B♭) 1 2
3
pp
p
2 p
Bsn. 1 2
1 Solo
p
Hn. (F) 1 2
1
mf p
3 4
Tpt. (B♭) 1 2
Tbn. 1 2
B. Tbn.
Tba.
Timp.
Vln. Solo
3
6
p
Vln. I
Vln. II
Vla.
pp
Vc.
Cb.

18

26

136
molto rit.
Tempo primo - solenne
Fl.
Ob.
Solo
pp
C. A.
Cl. (B♭)
Bsn.
Hn. (F)
1 Solo
p
Tpt. (B♭)
Tbn.
B. Tbn.
Tba.
Timp.
molto rit.
Tempo primo - solenne
Vln. I
div.
p sonore
Vln. II
div.
p sonore
Vla.
div.
pp
unis.
p sonore
Vc.
pp
div.
p sonore
Cb.
pp
p sonore